SHORT RUNS,

The blueprint to unleashing Profits in digital label printing

BIG GAINS

SHORT RUNS,

The blueprint to unleashing Profits in digital label printing

BIG GAINS

Ashok Gupta & Archit Gupta

Worldwide Published by
Pendown Press

PENDOWN PRESS LLP
An ISO 9001 & ISO 14001 Certified Co.,
Regd. Office: 3767A, Kanhaiya Nagar,
Tri Nagar, Delhi-110035
Ph.: 8130886000, 9650072927
E-mail: info@pendownpress.com
Branch Office: 1A/2A, 20, Hari Sadan, Ansari Road,
Daryaganj, New Delhi-110002
Ph.: 011-45794768
Website: PendownPress.com

Edition: 2024
Price: ₹ 399
ISBN: 978-93-6338-130-8

Layout and Cover Designed by Pendown Graphics Team
Printed and Bound in India by Thomson Press India Ltd.

To all passionate individuals who believe in the power of the Digital Printing Process to influence the users' needs & desires.

Contents

Resources and Further Reading

Acknowledgements

This book is dedicated to the most significant people in my life, who have shaped my journey in countless ways!

First and foremost, I wish to honor my parents, Sh. RS Gupta ji & Smt. Sushila Gupta ji. Without them, my existence in this world would not have been possible. To write about them feels like embarking on a never-ending tale, each deserving a book of their own. They have always stood as my pillars, even before the eyes of the divine.

My father is a remarkable soul who navigated the toughest times with resilience. Born into a humble family background, he, along with his elder brother & father, worked hard to carve out a niche in his field.

To my mother, Smt. Sushila Gupta, who weathered her own storms with unyielding resilience. From a very humble beginning to shouldering the responsibilities of managing our household, her journey has been one of unwavering determination and boundless love. Her nurturing presence transformed our house into a sanctuary of warmth and love. As both "Mummy" to me and "Dadi" to my sons, she remains the cornerstone of our lives, embodying strength, compassion, and boundless love.

To my sisters, who have been my unwavering support. Your presence in my life has been nothing short of a blessing. Thank you for being you! Without you being you, I would never be ME!

To all my friends, colleagues, and supporters — your unwavering belief in me has fueled my journey and made this book a reality.

To my friend Dinesh Verma, CEO of Pendown Press, and his team for their support and suggestions throughout the creative process.

To all my loved ones who have been with me on this journey—thank you for your unwavering support, encouragement, and love. Even if your names are not mentioned, you will always hold a special place in my heart.

Lastly, but most importantly, to my wife, Shalini, for tolerating my antics for over three decades. She continues to be my source of strength and inspiration. From the depths of my heart, I express my deepest gratitude and love, knowing that she is the anchor that steadies my ship through life's tempests. Love you...

With love and gratitude,

Ashok Gupta

❍ ❍ ❍ ❍

Preface

Welcome to *Short Runs, Big Gains: The Blueprint to Unleashing Profits in Digital Label Printing*. In today's fast-paced market, where speed and customization are paramount, digital label printing has become a game-changer. *Did you know that the global digital label printing market is projected to grow at a compound annual growth rate (CAGR) of over 6% in the next few years?* This is not just a trend—it's a revolution transforming how businesses approach printing.

In this book, we'll delve into the world of digital label sheets, exploring their unique advantages and how they can turn short-run printing into a strategic advantage. Digital printing offers incredible flexibility, allowing businesses to produce high-quality labels in smaller quantities, tailored to specific needs. This ability to customize and adapt quickly can be the difference between leading the market and falling behind.

You'll discover how to tackle common challenges, such as high minimum order quantities and limited flexibility, and turn them into opportunities for growth. We'll also look at how leveraging digital label sheets can enhance your product offerings, drive higher profit margins, and prepare your business for future trends.

Ready to level up your printing game? Let's dive into the world of digital label printing and unlock new possibilities for your business.

Purpose of the Book

This book is designed to guide you through the dynamic world of digital label printing, focusing on how short-run solutions can drive your business forward. Here's what you'll gain:

1. **Uncover the Basics:** Understand the fundamentals of digital printing and how it can benefit your business, especially for short-run projects.
2. **Solve Key Challenges:** Learn how to tackle common issues in short-run printing with innovative strategies and practical tips.
3. **Spot Opportunities:** Discover how to leverage the latest trends to grow your market presence and cater to niche demands.
4. **Enhance Your Operations:** Gain insights into using digital label sheets to improve speed, quality, and cost-efficiency.
5. **Prepare for the Future:** Stay ahead with knowledge on emerging trends and how to adapt to evolving industry standards.

This book is your roadmap to mastering digital label printing and achieving significant business growth.

Who Should Read This Book?

The target readers for a book on digital label printing and its impact on label buyers could include:

1. **Label Manufacturers:** Professionals and companies involved in the production of labels who want to understand the benefits and challenges of digital printing technology.
2. **Marketing Professionals:** Individuals responsible for branding and marketing who need to understand how digital label printing can enhance their promotional strategies.
3. **Business Owners:** Small to medium-sized businesses looking to optimize their packaging and labeling processes for cost-effectiveness and efficiency.
4. **Supply Chain and Procurement Managers:** Those involved in the purchasing of labels who seek to understand how digital printing can impact supply chain decisions.
5. **Graphic Designers:** Designers who create label artwork and want to learn more about the capabilities and limitations of digital printing technologies.
6. **Consumers and End Users:** Individuals interested in the impact of digital labels on product presentation, sustainability, and consumer choices.
7. **Industry Analysts:** Researchers and analysts who study market trends, innovations, and consumer behaviors in the label industry.

8. **Educators and Students:** Professors and students in fields related to printing technology, marketing, and packaging design who seek comprehensive insights into modern label printing practices.

By catering to these groups, the book can provide valuable insights into how digital printing is transforming the label industry and its effects on various stakeholders.

Chapter 1

Introduction

The Indian printing industry has undergone a remarkable transformation in recent years, with digital printing emerging as a dominant force. While traditional offset printing has struggled to keep up with the fast-paced demands of modern businesses, digital printing offers a more flexible, efficient, and cost-effective solution.

India's diverse economy and rapidly growing consumer base provide an ideal environment for digital printing to thrive. Small and medium-sized enterprises (SMEs), which form the backbone of the Indian economy, often require printing solutions that can adapt to their fluctuating needs. Digital printing's ability to produce high-quality prints in smaller quantities without excessive setup costs makes it a perfect fit for these businesses.

One of the key advantages of digital printing in India is its ability to meet short-run demands. Unlike offset printing, which typically requires large print runs to be economically viable, digital printing allows businesses to produce smaller quantities without compromising on quality. This is particularly valuable in a market where product life cycles are shorter and customization is increasingly important.

Sustainability is flourishing in India's digital printing sector, with businesses adopting eco-friendly practices to benefit the planet. Digital printing minimizes waste and carbon footprints, helping companies meet regulations and the growing demand for greener products. This era brings exciting positive change and optimism for a sustainable future!

Emerging Trends in Short-Run Printing

Several key trends are shaping the future of short-run printing in India:

- **On-Demand Printing:** The Indian consumer is becoming increasingly sophisticated, demanding products that cater to their unique tastes and preferences. Short-run printing, with its ability to produce customized labels, packaging, and promotional materials in small batches, is the perfect solution to meet this demand. From FMCG to retail and e-commerce, businesses are leveraging personalization to build stronger customer relationships and drive sales.
- **Variable Data Printing:** This technology allows for the personalization of each printed piece with unique data, such as names, addresses, or product information. This is particularly valuable for targeted marketing campaigns and direct mail initiatives.
- **Integration with E-commerce:** Digital printing is playing a crucial role in supporting e-commerce businesses by enabling the efficient production of product catalogs, packaging, and other marketing materials.
- **Sustainable Printing:** People and businesses in India are becoming more and more worried about the environment. Short-run digital printing is better for the environment than traditional printing. This is because it wastes less paper by printing only what you need. Also, people are using inks and materials that are better for the planet.

- **Cost Efficiency and Flexibility:** One of the most significant advantages of short-run digital printing is its cost efficiency. For Indian businesses, especially SMEs, the ability to produce only what is needed, without the need for large print runs, is a major advantage. This not only reduces inventory costs but also allows for greater flexibility in responding to market changes. The ability to make last-minute changes to designs or to produce limited editions without incurring high costs is a key benefit that is driving the adoption of short-run printing in India.

Conclusion

Digital printing in India is rapidly changing the game, especially for small and medium-sized businesses that need quick, cost-effective, and high-quality solutions. As customization and sustainability become more important, short-run printing is emerging as a key trend, allowing businesses to meet specific demands without large print runs. We will explore more about these exciting opportunities and innovations in the upcoming chapters, so get ready!

Chapter 2

Problem Statement: Challenges in Short-Run Printing

While short-run printing has revolutionized the Indian printing industry, it's not without its challenges. In this chapter, we'll take a deep dive into the obstacles that businesses face when using this innovative approach, especially compared to traditional printing methods.

Cost Implications of Traditional Methods

Traditional printing methods, such as offset printing, have long been the standard in the industry. While these methods are efficient for large-volume print jobs, they become costly and inefficient for smaller runs. The initial setup costs, including the creation of printing plates and the time-consuming process of aligning and calibrating machines, make traditional printing prohibitively expensive for short-run jobs. Businesses that require smaller quantities often find themselves paying a premium, as the per-unit cost is significantly higher when spread over fewer units.

This is especially tough for small and medium-sized businesses in India, which often have limited budgets, and where every rupee counts. The high costs of traditional printing can discourage these businesses from offering customized products to their customers, limiting their options.

Limitations in Product Customization and Flexibility

While short-run printing is praised for its ability to cater to customized orders, it still faces limitations in terms of the level of customization and flexibility it can offer.

- **Complexity in Managing Multiple Designs:** Short-run printing is praised for its ability to handle customized orders, but managing multiple designs, colors, and formats within a single order can be challenging. The complexity increases with the number of variations, leading to potential inefficiencies in the production process. This complexity can slow down turnaround times, which is particularly problematic in industries where speed is critical.
- **Resource Strain:** Customization in short-run printing often requires specialized equipment and skilled personnel, both of which may be in limited supply. Businesses without the latest technology or experienced staff may struggle to meet the customization demands of short-run printing, potentially leading to lower quality output or delayed orders.
- **Turnaround Time Issues:** While short-run printing generally offers quicker turnaround times compared to traditional methods, the need for high levels of customization can slow down the process. Extensive customization requires careful attention to detail, which can extend production timelines and limit a business's ability to be flexible in meeting urgent customer demands. This can be a significant drawback in competitive markets where speed and agility are critical to maintaining customer satisfaction and loyalty.

High Minimum Order Quantities and Their Impact

In short-run printing, businesses often encounter challenges related to meeting high Minimum Order Quantities (MOQs). These challenges can have significant implications on costs, inventory management, and a company's ability to innovate. Let's explore the key issues associated with high MOQs:

- **Pressure to Meet MOQs:** Despite the advantages of short-run printing, businesses may still face pressures to meet specific minimum order quantities (MOQs) to justify production costs. This requirement can be a barrier for companies that only need a small quantity of a particular product or want to test a new design without committing to a large production run.
- **Overproduction Risks:** Meeting high MOQs can lead to overproduction, resulting in excess inventory that may not be sold. This not only ties up capital but also increases storage costs and the risk of waste. For SMEs, the financial burden of unsold inventory can be significant, affecting cash flow and overall profitability.
- **Limited Experimentation:** High MOQs can restrict a business's ability to experiment with new products or marketing strategies. The need to commit to a larger quantity than necessary can deter innovation and prevent businesses from responding quickly to market trends or customer preferences.

Conclusion

While short-run printing offers businesses the flexibility and customization they need to meet today's demands, it's not without its challenges. Higher per-unit costs, the complexity of managing multiple designs, and the pressure to meet high minimum order quantities can all impact profitability and efficiency.

In the following chapters, we'll explore strategies and solutions to help you overcome these hurdles. We'll provide insights and tools to help you maximize the benefits of short-run printing while minimizing its drawbacks. Get ready to discover how you can succeed in the dynamic world of digital printing.

❍ ❍ ❍ ❍

Chapter 3

The Rise of Short-Run Opportunities

As the market evolves, the demand for personalized and small-batch products has surged, opening new avenues for businesses to thrive. Short-run printing has emerged as a powerful tool to meet these evolving consumer preferences and capitalize on niche markets. In this chapter, we will explore the growing opportunities that short-run printing presents and how businesses can leverage these advantages to gain a competitive edge.

Market Demand for Personalized and Small-Batch Products

- **Increasing Consumer Desire for Personalization:** Consumers today want products that are personalized to their preferences. They want items that are unique and tailored to their individual tastes. This desire for personalization is driving the demand for customized products, such as custom labels, packaging, and marketing materials. Traditional mass production methods often can't meet this demand for uniqueness. That's where short-run printing comes in. It allows businesses to produce customized products in smaller quantities, catering to specific customer needs. With short-run printing, businesses can create personalized products without the limitations of large print runs.

- **Growth of E-Commerce and Direct-to-Consumer Models:** The growth of e-commerce and direct-to-consumer (DTC) models has significantly contributed to the increasing demand for personalized and small-batch products. Online platforms have made it more convenient for consumers to discover and purchase customized items. At the same time, businesses can leverage data-driven insights to understand individual preferences and provide products that align with them. Short-run printing is a perfect fit for this evolving landscape. It allows businesses to swiftly adapt to changing consumer trends and preferences, enabling them to meet the demand for personalized products promptly.
- **Adaptation to Fast-Paced Market Trends:** The market changes fast, and consumers are always changing their minds. Businesses need to be quick and flexible to keep up. Short-run printing is the perfect for this. It allows businesses to quickly create and test new products, designs, or marketing materials without committing to large quantities. This agility is essential for staying competitive and meeting the needs of consumers who want new and unique products.

Advantages of Short Runs for Niche Markets and Limited Editions

- **Niche Markets:** A Sweet Spot for Short-Run Printing: Short-run printing is a great tool for businesses targeting niche markets. These markets often need specialized products that cater to specific interests or groups of people. By producing limited quantities of tailored products, businesses can better serve these niche segments and become leaders in their specialized areas. This approach not only builds customer loyalty but also helps businesses avoid overproducing and wasting products.

- **Opportunity for Limited Editions:** Short-run printing opens up a world of opportunity for businesses to create exclusive products that ignite excitement and drive demand. Imagine collectible labels, unique packaging, or special promotional materials that are only available in limited quantities. This strategy adds a touch of exclusivity, making customers eager to get their hands on these one-of-a-kind items. The sense of urgency encourages swift purchasing decisions, resulting in a boost in sales.
- **Reduced Risk, Increased Flexibility:** Short-run printing lets businesses try out new ideas and products without taking big financial risks. This flexibility allows companies to test how customers react to new things, get feedback, and improve their products based on what they learn. It also allows for more frequent updates and innovations, keeping products fresh and up-to-date.

Conclusion

Short-run printing is becoming more popular, and it's a great opportunity for printing businesses. By offering personalized and small-quantity products, printing companies can make more money, serve specific customers, and create special, limited-edition items. In the next chapters, we'll talk about how to use these opportunities and make short-run printing work well for your business. We'll give you practical tips and ideas to help you succeed.

Chapter 4

Innovative Solutions with Digital Label Sheets

Digital label sheets represent a significant advancement in the world of printing, offering unique solutions to traditional challenges and opening new possibilities for businesses. In this chapter, we delve into the world of digital label sheets and examine how they overcome the limitations of conventional printing methods. Get ready to discover the exciting advancements that digital label sheets bring to the table!

Introduction to Digital Label Sheets and Their Unique Properties

- **What Are Digital Label Sheets?** Digital label sheets are a versatile and innovative printing solution that combines the benefits of digital printing with the functionality of traditional label sheets. These sheets are designed to be compatible with various label printers and offer a wide range of customizable options.
  - **Versatility:** One of the standout features of digital label sheets is their versatility. It can be used for a wide range of applications, including:
  - **Product labeling:** Labeling various products such as food items, pharmaceuticals, and consumer goods.
  - **Barcode printing:** Creating barcodes for inventory management, tracking, and point-of-sale applications.

- **Promotional materials:** Designing labels for promotional items like stickers, gift tags, and event badges.
- **Shipping labels:** Printing shipping labels with address information, tracking numbers, and other relevant details.

➢ **High-Quality Output:** Digital label sheets are known for their ability to produce high-quality prints with consistent color accuracy and sharp details. Advanced digital printing technologies ensure that each label is printed with precision, resulting in a professional finish that enhances the overall appearance of the product.

➢ **Integration:** Digital label sheets can be easily integrated into existing production workflows, providing a seamless solution for businesses of all sizes. They can be compatible with various label printers and software systems, making it easy to incorporate them into your operations.

➢ **On-Demand Printing Capabilities:** Digital label sheets excel in on-demand printing, allowing businesses to produce labels as needed without the constraints of large minimum order quantities. This capability supports small-batch production and customization, enabling businesses to respond quickly to changing market demands and customer preferences.

➢ **Scalability and Flexibility of Digital Label Sheets:** Digital Label Sheets offer excellent scalability, allowing businesses to easily adjust production volumes based on demand. Whether it's a small batch for a niche market or a larger run for a more extensive campaign, Digital Label Sheets provide the flexibility to scale operations without significant additional costs.

"Bada karo, jaldi kamao!" The ability to scale up or down as needed ensures that businesses can optimize production to match market demand, avoiding the costs associated with overproduction or underutilization of resources.

How Digital Label Sheets Address Traditional Printing Challenges

- **Reducing Setup and Prepress Costs:** Traditional label printing often involves complex setup processes, including the creation of printing plates and other prepress tasks. Digital label sheets eliminate these setup costs by using digital files directly for printing. This reduction in prepress expenses makes digital label sheets a cost-effective solution, particularly for short-run and customized orders.
- **Minimizing Waste and Overproduction:** Conventional label printing methods can result in significant waste due to excess production and obsolete designs. Digital label sheets mitigate this issue by allowing for precise print runs, which reduces the risk of overproduction and minimizes waste. This efficiency not only benefits the environment but also helps businesses manage inventory more effectively.
- **Enhancing Flexibility and Speed:** The flexibility of digital label sheets enables businesses to quickly adjust designs, make last-minute changes, and produce labels with variable data. This adaptability is a major advantage over traditional methods, where changes can be costly and time-consuming. Digital label sheets streamline the production process, allowing for faster turnaround times and greater responsiveness to market trends.

- **Facilitating Personalization and Customization:** Traditional printing methods often struggle with the complexity of producing personalized or customized labels. Digital label sheets excel in this area by easily accommodating variable data and individualized designs. Businesses can offer personalized labels with unique names, codes, or images, enhancing the appeal of their products and meeting specific customer requirements.

Conclusion

In conclusion, digital label sheets offer a valuable solution for businesses seeking to improve their labeling processes. They offer innovative solutions to traditional challenges and provide businesses with a powerful tool to optimize their label production processes. With their versatility, high-quality output, and on-demand capabilities, digital label sheets are a must-have for any business looking to enhance their printing operations. In the upcoming chapter, we will explore practical applications of digital label sheets and share actionable strategies to help you make the most of their benefits. Get ready to unlock the full potential of digital label sheets and take your business offerings to the next level!

❍ ❍ ❍ ❍

Chapter 5

Product Features and Benefits

Digital label sheets are changing the game in the label printing industry, offering a mix of speed, quality, and flexibility that solves many traditional printing problems. This chapter will dive into the standout features of digital label sheets and their benefits. We'll explore how these sheets provide quick, high-quality labels and the advantages of zero minimum order quantities (MOQs) while delivering mass-produced quality.

"Quick Labels, Real Feel": Speed and Quality in Label Printing

1. **Rapid Production Turnaround:** One of the biggest advantages of digital label sheets is their super-fast production turnaround. Traditional label printing methods involve long setup times, like plate-making and registration adjustments, which can slow things down. Digital printing skips these prepress steps by using digital files directly, which means labels can be printed quickly and efficiently.

   In markets where speed is crucial—think retail and e-commerce—the ability to get high-quality labels in no time is a game-changer. For example, if you have a seasonal promotion or a last-minute offer, digital label sheets can help you get your products ready quickly. This fast production keeps you ahead of the curve and ensures you meet tight deadlines with ease.

2. **Consistent High-Quality Output:** Digital label sheets are designed to produce consistently top-notch prints. Thanks to advanced digital printing technology, you get high resolution and accurate colors every time. This means that your labels will always look sharp and vibrant, which is essential for maintaining a professional and appealing product appearance.

   For brands that focus on visual appeal, like luxury or premium products, the high quality of digital labels is a huge plus. With digital label sheets, you get that premium look and feel, which helps your products stand out and attract customers. You can achieve this level of quality without the limitations of traditional printing methods.

3. **Flexibility in Design and Customization:** Digital label sheets shine when it comes to flexibility and customization. Unlike traditional printing, which requires extensive setup for each new design, digital printing handles intricate designs and variable data effortlessly. This flexibility allows you to create labels with detailed graphics, unique text, and even personalized elements.

   This level of customization is a huge advantage in today's market. Whether you're looking to personalize labels for a special promotion or adapt designs based on the latest trends, digital label sheets make it easy. For instance, a business can quickly produce customized labels for a limited-edition product, boosting engagement and sales with personalized touches.

4. **Efficient Short-Run Production:** Digital label sheets are perfect for short-run production. Traditional methods often require large quantities to be cost-effective, leading to excess inventory and higher costs for smaller batches. Digital

printing lets you print exactly what you need, reducing waste and minimizing storage needs.

Short-run production is great for scenarios like testing new products, running seasonal promotions, or handling special orders. For example, if you're launching a new product and want to test market response, digital label sheets allow you to print a small batch without the risk of overproduction. This efficient approach helps you adapt quickly and manage your resources better.

"Zero MOQ with Mass-Produced Quality": Elevating Product Presentation Without Excess Inventory

1. **Eliminating Minimum Order Quantities:** One of the most attractive features of digital label sheets is their ability to eliminate minimum order quantities (MOQs). Traditional printing often requires large quantities to make the process cost-effective, which can be a barrier for businesses needing smaller quantities or wanting to try out new designs.

   Digital label sheets make it possible to print just what you need. Whether it's a few hundred or a few thousand labels, digital printing accommodates various order sizes without extra costs or setup. This flexibility helps businesses avoid the financial strain of large MOQs and manage their production more efficiently.

2. **Elevating Product Presentation:** The quality of digital label sheets significantly enhances product presentation. Labels are crucial for branding and consumer perception, and high-quality digital labels ensure a premium look and feel.

Businesses can use this to create visually striking labels that stand out on shelves and grab customer attention.

For premium products or specialty items, high-quality labels help maintain a top-tier image and differentiate from competitors. With digital label sheets, you get the quality that reflects the value of your products, reinforcing your brand identity and making a lasting impression on customers.

3. **Reducing Waste and Managing Inventory:** Digital label sheets are a great way to manage inventory and cut down on waste. By allowing on-demand production, these sheets help businesses avoid overproduction and the risks of excess inventory. This approach not only saves on storage costs but also supports more sustainable practices by reducing waste.

   With zero MOQ requirements, you can align your production with actual demand. For example, if you need labels for a specific promotion or seasonal item, you can produce them as needed without the worry of unsold inventory. This efficient management of resources contributes to better financial performance and supports environmental sustainability.

4. **Enabling Quick Changes and Updates:** The flexibility of digital label sheets extends to making quick changes and updates to label designs. Traditional printing often involves extra costs and delays for modifying designs. Digital printing removes these barriers by allowing easy adjustments to designs, product information, or last-minute changes.

   This capability is especially useful in fast-moving markets where regulations, trends, or consumer preferences change rapidly. Businesses can quickly adapt their labels to new requirements or market trends, staying competitive and responsive to customer needs without incurring significant delays or expenses.

Conclusion

Digital label sheets offer a range of features and benefits that enhance the label printing process. With their rapid production capabilities, consistent high-quality output, and flexibility in design and customization, they provide a powerful tool for modern printing businesses. The elimination of minimum order quantities and improved product presentation further enhances their appeal.

❍ ❍ ❍ ❍

Chapter 6

Maximizing Profit Margins with Efficient Practices

While the initial investment in digital label printing equipment may seem significant, the long-term cost savings can be substantial. This chapter explores the cost-benefit analysis of using digital label sheets and provides practical tips for reducing waste and boosting productivity.

Cost-Benefit Analysis of Using Digital Label Sheets

1. **Initial Investment vs. Long-Term Savings:** When considering digital label sheets, it's important to weigh the initial investment against the long-term savings. While digital printing equipment and materials may come with a higher upfront cost compared to traditional methods, the benefits in terms of efficiency, reduced waste, and flexibility often outweigh these initial expenses.

   "Shuruat mein lagta hai zyada, lekin baad mein faida bada hota hai!" Digital label sheets eliminate the need for costly setup processes associated with traditional printing. This means you can produce high-quality labels quickly and without incurring extra costs for setup or plates. Over time, these savings add up, making digital printing a cost-effective solution in the long run.

2. **Reducing Overheads with On-Demand Production**
    - **Printing Just What You Need:** Digital label sheets let you print labels as needed, which saves you money. With traditional printing, you often need to print a lot to make it affordable, which can lead to having too many labels. Digital printing helps you avoid this by letting you print only what you need.
    - **Save Money, Stay Lean:** By printing just what you need, you don't have to tie up your money in labels you might not sell. This is great for your cash flow and helps you run a leaner business. Being able to quickly adjust to changes without having too many labels is a big advantage for managing your costs.
3. **Eliminating Setup and Plate Costs:** One of the significant benefits of digital label sheets is the elimination of setup and plate costs. Traditional printing methods require the creation of plates and extensive setup time, which adds to the overall cost of production. Digital printing bypasses these requirements, leading to lower costs per print job.

    "Plate aur setup ka chakkar khatam!" With digital label sheets, you can immediately start production without the need for costly and time-consuming setup processes. This reduction in setup costs contributes to better profit margins, especially for smaller print runs where traditional methods would be less cost-effective.
4. **Monitoring and Adjustments for Optimal Efficiency:** Continuous improvement is key to maximizing profit margins. "Nazariya banaaye rakho, fayda aur badhega!" Regularly monitoring production processes and making adjustments where necessary can help businesses optimize their use of

Digital Label Sheets. This might include refining design layouts, improving staff training, or investing in upgraded technology to further enhance efficiency.

By focusing on continuous improvement, businesses can ensure that they are consistently operating at peak efficiency, maximizing their profit potential with Digital Label Sheets.

Tips for Reducing Waste and Enhancing Productivity

1. **Implementing Efficient Workflow Processes:**
    - **Make Things Easier, Get More Done:** To get more done and waste less, you need to make your work process better. Digital label sheets are flexible, but you still need to manage them well. Plan your work carefully, keep track of your supplies, and take care of your equipment. This will help you work faster and better.
    - **Work Smarter, Not Harder:** When you make your work process better, you spend less time and money on each job. This helps you get more done and waste less. Keep checking how you're working and make changes to improve things.
2. **Utilizing Digital Proofing and Quality Control:** Digital proofing is a key advantage of digital label sheets. By providing digital proofs before production, businesses can ensure that the final labels meet quality standards and reduce the likelihood of errors. This pre-production review helps in identifying and correcting issues before printing, saving time and resources.

    "Digital proofing se errors kam karo!" Quality control during the proofing stage prevents costly mistakes and reduces the

need for reprints. By catching potential issues early, you can avoid wasting materials and time on incorrect prints, thus improving overall efficiency and reducing waste.

3. **Optimizing Material Usage:** Effective material usage is crucial for minimizing waste. Digital label sheets are designed to maximize material efficiency, but it's important to make sure that materials are used optimally. For example, arranging multiple labels on a single sheet and ensuring that there are minimal gaps can help in making the most of each material.

   "Material ko optimize karo, waste kam karo!" By carefully planning and arranging your label designs, you can reduce material waste and lower production costs. Efficient use of materials not only contributes to cost savings but also supports more sustainable printing practices.

4. **Adopting On-Demand Production Strategies:**
   - **Print Only What You Need:** When you print labels only when you need them, you're not only saving money but also reducing waste. Instead of making more labels than you need and having to store them, you can produce them on demand, ensuring that you have just the right amount.
   - **Leaner Operations, Higher Profits:** Adopting an on-demand production strategy helps you run a leaner operation. By avoiding excess inventory, you free up capital and reduce storage costs. This means more money for your business and higher profits. Additionally, producing labels only when needed aligns your production with actual demand, improving overall efficiency and reducing the risk of unsold inventory.

5. **Investing in Employee Training:** Proper training for employees is essential for enhancing productivity and

reducing waste. Ensure that your team is well-trained in operating digital printing equipment, managing workflows, and maintaining quality control. Knowledgeable and skilled employees are more likely to work efficiently and produce high-quality results.

"Training se productivity badhao!" Investing in employee training not only improves operational efficiency but also contributes to higher quality outputs and reduced waste. Well-trained staff can better handle the complexities of digital label printing and contribute to smoother, more efficient operations.

Conclusion

Maximizing profit margins in the digital label printing industry involves a strategic approach to leveraging the benefits of digital label sheets while implementing efficient practices. By understanding the cost-benefit analysis and adopting practices to reduce waste and enhance productivity, businesses can significantly improve their profitability.

In the next chapter, we will explore the future trends in label printing. Stay tuned as we dive deeper into these developments and uncover more strategies to maximize the potential of digital label sheets. Get ready to unlock new opportunities and drive growth in your business with the insights that lie ahead.

Chapter 7

Future of Printing: Staying Ahead with Innovation

The printing industry is changing fast. New technology and what people want are changing how things are printed. To stay successful, businesses need to keep up with these changes. In this chapter, we'll talk about the future of printing and how innovation can help you stay ahead.

Upcoming Trends and Technologies in Label Printing

1. **Digital Printing Advancements:** The digital printing landscape is evolving rapidly, with innovations that promise to transform the way labels are produced. Future advancements in digital printing will likely focus on enhancing speed, precision, and color accuracy. High-resolution digital presses capable of producing near-offset quality will become more accessible, allowing businesses to offer top-tier products without the high costs traditionally associated with such quality.

   "Jaldi aur behtareen chhapayi ka zamana aa raha hai!" With these advancements, businesses can expect faster production times, reduced costs, and a wider range of customizable options, giving them a competitive edge in the market.

2. **Smart Labels and Interactive Packaging:** The rise of smart labels and interactive packaging is another trend set to

revolutionize the industry. These labels are equipped with QR codes, NFC chips, and augmented reality features that engage consumers in new and exciting ways. Brands can offer customers more information about the product, special promotions, or even an immersive experience through their labels.

"Smart labels se nayi duniya ka darwaza kholenge!" As consumers become more tech-savvy, the demand for such interactive features will grow, making smart labels an essential part of any forward-thinking printing business.

3. **Eco-Friendly and Sustainable Printing:** Sustainability is no longer just a trend; it's becoming a requirement. The future of label printing will see a continued emphasis on eco-friendly practices, from the use of biodegradable materials to water-based inks and energy-efficient printing processes.

   "Har chhapaayi ab hogi paryavaran ke saath!" By adopting these practices, businesses can not only meet regulatory requirements but also appeal to the growing segment of environmentally conscious consumers, thereby gaining a significant market advantage.

4. **Automation and AI Integration:** The integration of automation and artificial intelligence (AI) into label printing processes is set to change the industry dramatically. From automated design tools that help create labels faster to AI-driven quality control systems that ensure each label meets exacting standards, these technologies will make production more efficient and cost-effective.

   "AI aur automation se production hoga super-fast!" This shift will allow businesses to reduce manual labor, minimize errors, and streamline workflows, ultimately leading to higher profit margins.

5. **Digital Twin Technology:** Digital twin technology, which involves creating a virtual replica of physical products, is gaining traction in various industries, including printing. This technology can be used to simulate label designs and production processes before they are executed, allowing businesses to test different options and identify potential issues without wasting resources.

   "Digital twins se sab kuch pehle se predict kar paayenge!" This capability not only enhances efficiency but also enables businesses to offer highly customized and accurate label solutions to their clients.

Preparing for Future Shifts in Consumer Demands and Industry Standards

1. **Adapting to Consumer Preferences:** As consumer preferences continue to evolve, businesses must stay agile and ready to adapt. The demand for personalization and customization is expected to grow, with consumers seeking products that reflect their individual tastes and lifestyles. Businesses that can offer these personalized experiences will be better positioned to capture market share.

   "Consumer ka demand badalta hai, humein bhi badalna padega!" To stay ahead, it's crucial to continuously monitor consumer trends and adjust your offerings accordingly.

2. **Compliance with Industry Standards:** With stricter regulations on labeling and packaging, particularly in sectors like food, pharmaceuticals, and cosmetics, businesses must ensure that their products comply with the latest industry standards. Staying informed about these changes and integrating them into your production processes will be key to

avoiding costly compliance issues.

"Naye standards ke saath chalte raho, aur samay se pehle taiyaar ho jao!" By proactively addressing these standards, you can prevent disruptions in your operations and maintain a strong market presence.

3. **Building Resilience in Supply Chains:** Building resilience in supply chains is crucial for businesses to thrive in the face of disruptions like the COVID-19 pandemic. To achieve this, it is important to diversify suppliers, adopt just-in-time inventory practices, and leverage digital tools for supply chain management. By implementing these strategies, businesses can ensure continuity and reduce risks associated with global events or shifts in consumer demand. Remember, a strong supply chain leads to a strong business!

4. **Build Strong Relationships**

   Enhance Supplier Partnerships:

   - Maintain open and regular communication with suppliers.
   - Collaborate on problem-solving and negotiate better terms for improved efficiency and cost savings.

   Strengthen Customer Connections:

   - Offer personalized services and gather feedback to improve your offerings.
   - Implement loyalty programs to encourage repeat business and strengthen customer loyalty.

   Collaborate with Industry Partners:

   - Network with industry associations and technology providers to gain insights and opportunities.

- Engage in joint ventures and projects to access new markets and innovations.

5. **Leveraging Data for Strategic Decision-Making :** Data will play an increasingly important role in shaping the future of label printing. By leveraging data analytics, businesses can gain insights into consumer behavior, optimize production processes, and make more informed decisions about product development and marketing strategies.

   "Data ke bal par business decisions ko aur mazboot banao!" Utilizing data effectively will enable you to stay ahead of the competition and capitalize on emerging opportunities.

Conclusion

The future of label printing is bright, filled with opportunities for those who are willing to innovate and adapt. By staying ahead of technological trends, meeting the evolving demands of consumers, and preparing for changes in industry standards, your business can thrive in this dynamic environment.

Chapter 8

Conclusion

As we wrap up our exploration of the digital label printing industry, let's review the key insights and strategic takeaways from each chapter:

Recap of Key Points and Strategic Takeaways

1. **Introduction**
   - **Overview of the Digital Printing Landscape:** We examined how digital printing has transformed the industry, providing a more flexible, efficient, and cost-effective solution compared to traditional methods. The rise of digital technology has reshaped the market, offering new opportunities for businesses to meet evolving demands.
   - **Emerging Trends in Short-Run Printing:** We explored the growing trend of short-run printing, which caters to the need for smaller quantities and quicker turnaround times. This approach is particularly advantageous for businesses aiming to adapt quickly to market changes and customer preferences.
2. **Problem Statement: Challenges in Short-Run Printing**
   - **Cost Implications of Traditional Methods:** We identified how traditional methods can be cost-prohibitive for short-run printing, emphasizing the benefits of digital solutions that reduce setup costs and waste.

- **Limitations in Product Customization and Flexibility:** The complexities of managing multiple designs and variations in short-run printing were discussed, highlighting how digital label sheets offer enhanced flexibility and customization.
- **High Minimum Order Quantities and Their Impact:** We examined the challenges of high MOQs and how they can lead to overproduction and excess inventory. Digital label sheets address these issues by allowing for lower quantities and reducing inventory costs.

3. **The Rise of Short-Run Opportunities**
   - **Market Demand for Personalized and Small-Batch Products:** We discussed the increasing consumer demand for personalized and small-batch products, which short-run printing can efficiently meet. This trend presents significant opportunities for businesses to cater to niche markets.
   - **Advantages of Short Runs for Niche Markets and Limited Editions:** Short-run printing provides the flexibility to create unique and limited-edition products, allowing businesses to tap into niche markets and enhance their product offerings.
4. **Innovative Solutions with Digital Label Sheets**
   - **Introduction to Digital Label Sheets and Their Unique Properties:** We introduced digital label sheets as a revolutionary solution in the printing industry, offering high-quality, customizable labels with minimal setup and waste.

- **How Digital Label Sheets Address Traditional Printing Challenges:** We explored how digital label sheets overcome traditional printing challenges by providing enhanced flexibility, faster turnaround times, and reduced waste.

5. **Product Features and Benefits**
    - **"Quick Labels, Real Feel":** The chapter highlighted how digital label sheets deliver fast and high-quality label printing, meeting the needs for speed and precision in today's market.
    - **"Zero MOQ with Mass-Produced Quality":** We discussed how digital label sheets enable businesses to produce high-quality labels without the constraints of high MOQs, allowing for better product presentation and reduced excess inventory.
6. **Maximizing Profit Margins with Efficient Practices**
    - **Cost-Benefit Analysis of Using Digital Label Sheets:** We analyzed the financial advantages of adopting digital label sheets, emphasizing how they can improve profitability through cost savings and increased efficiency.
    - **Tips for Reducing Waste and Enhancing Productivity:** Practical tips were provided for minimizing waste and boosting productivity, ensuring that businesses can maximize their profit margins with digital label sheets.
7. **Future of Printing: Staying Ahead with Innovation**
    - **Upcoming Trends and Technologies in Label Printing:** We looked at the future trends and emerging

technologies in label printing, preparing businesses to adapt to ongoing innovations in the industry.

- **Preparing for Future Shifts in Consumer Demands and Industry Standards:** The chapter discussed how to stay ahead of shifting consumer demands and evolving industry standards by embracing innovation and strategic practices.

Get ready for the future of printing!" As you move forward, use these ideas to grow your business. Be open to new things, stay up-to-date, and always look for ways to improve. The future of label printing is bright, and with the right approach, you can achieve great success.

Encouragement to Adopt Innovative Solutions

As we wrap up our journey through the world of digital label printing, we want to share a little personal note with you. The insights we've explored together offer a powerful roadmap for transforming your business. Embracing innovative solutions like digital label sheets isn't just about keeping up with the latest trends; it's about positioning yourself at the forefront of the industry.

"Nayi technologies aur strategies ko apnaane ka samay aa gaya hai!" By adopting these cutting-edge solutions, you're not just improving your processes—you're opening doors to new opportunities and greater success. Digital label sheets offer the flexibility, quality, and efficiency that can give your business the competitive edge it needs.

Remember, the journey of innovation is continuous. ***"Har naye trend aur technology ko samajhna aur apne business mein implement karna zaroori hai."*** So, take these insights and use them to drive your growth. Test new ideas, experiment with digital tools, and never shy away from exploring what's next.

The future is bright and full of possibilities. ***"Agar aap naye solutions ko apnate hain, toh aapki business growth ko koi nahi rok sakta."*** Stay curious, stay innovative, and keep pushing the boundaries. Your next big success could be just around the corner.

And Because We Care for You!

As we wrap up our exploration of the digital label printing industry, let's review the key insights and strategic takeaways from each chapter:

Chapter 9

How to Increase Profitability in the Business of Digital Printing of Labels

To increase profitability in a digital printing business focused on label production, consider the following strategies:

1. **Expand Product Range:** Diversify your offerings by including various types of labels such as specialty labels (e.g., waterproof, thermal), customized sizes, and eco-friendly options.
2. **Leverage Customization:** Utilize variable data printing to provide personalized labels for marketing campaigns, events, or special releases, which can command higher prices.
3. **Increase Operational Efficiency:** Streamline processes by investing in workflow automation and top-notch digital printing equipment to reduce waste, speed up production times, and improve quality.
4. **Target Niche Markets:** Identify and cater to specific industries that require unique labeling solutions, such as food and beverage, cosmetics, pharmaceuticals, or craft breweries.
5. **Enhance Marketing Efforts:** Utilize digital marketing strategies, including social media and search engine optimization (SEO), to reach a broader audience and showcase your unique offerings.

6. **Develop Strong Client Relationships:** Build long-term partnerships with clients through excellent service, timely delivery, and the ability to handle ongoing projects, ensuring repeat business.
7. **Implement Value-Added Services:** Offer design services, consultation on branding strategies, or integrated packaging solutions to provide more comprehensive offerings to clients.
8. **Utilize E-Commerce Platforms:** Set up an online ordering system or e-commerce site to make it easier for customers to place orders directly, increasing visibility and accessibility.
9. **Enhance Quality Control:** Maintain high printing quality to improve customer satisfaction and reputation, which can lead to referral business and repeat clients.
10. **Adopt Green Practices:** Embrace sustainability by offering eco-friendly labels and processes, appealing to environmentally conscious brands willing to pay premium prices.
11. **Optimize Pricing Strategies:** Reassess pricing models to ensure competitive yet profitable pricing while offering incentives for larger volume orders or long-term contracts.
12. **Participate in Industry Events:** Attend trade shows and exhibitions to network with potential clients, showcase your products, and stay informed about the latest trends and innovations in digital printing.

By employing these strategies, you can effectively enhance revenue streams and profitability in the competitive digital label printing market.

❍ ❍ ❍ ❍

Chapter 10

How to Beat Competition with Other Digital Printers of Labels

To beat the competition in the digital label printing industry, a digital printer can adopt various strategies focused on differentiation, efficiency, service, and innovation:

1. **Quality and Consistency:** Prioritize high-quality printing with consistent results. Invest in state-of-the-art printing technology and conduct rigorous quality control checks to ensure every product meets or exceeds customer expectations.
2. **Fast Turnaround Times:** Offer quicker production and delivery times than competitors. Streamline processes and leverage just-in-time manufacturing to fulfill urgent customer requests promptly.
3. **Customization and Personalization:** Provide advanced customization options through variable data printing, allowing clients to personalize labels for their products, enhancing their market appeal.
4. **Diverse Product Range:** Expand your product offerings to include various label types, materials, and finishes. Cater to niche markets such as food, beverage, cosmetics, and pharmaceuticals, which generally pay higher prices due to the nature of their business.

5. **Responsive Customer Service:** Build strong relationships with customers by offering exceptional service, responsiveness, and personalized attention. A customer-centric approach can foster loyalty and referral business.
6. **Innovative Solutions:** Continuously seek to innovate by exploring new materials, technologies, or designs. Stay ahead of industry trends to offer cutting-edge solutions that meet emerging needs.
7. **Adoption of Sustainable Practices:** Position your business as an environmentally responsible option by using eco-friendly materials and processes. Highlight these practices as a key selling point to attract environmentally conscious clients.
8. **Effective Marketing Strategies:** Utilize digital marketing techniques, including SEO, social media, and content marketing, to increase visibility and attract new customers. Showcase your unique selling points through engaging content.
9. **Value-Added Services:** Offer complementary services such as design assistance, inventory management, or shipping solutions to provide customers with a complete service package.
10. **Competitive Pricing:** Analyze competitors' pricing and adjust your pricing structure accordingly to offer competitive rates without compromising quality. Consider offering bulk discounts or loyalty programs.
11. **Customer Feedback and Improvement:** Regularly solicit customer feedback and make necessary adjustments to your services or products based on their inputs. Listening to

customers can help identify areas for improvement and reveal opportunities for innovation.

12. **Networking and Partnerships:** Build relationships with distributors, retailers, and other companies in your supply chain to enhance visibility and create new business opportunities.

Chapter 11

How to Select the Right Label Sheet

When selecting label sheets for digital printing, professionals should consider several key traits to ensure optimal performance and quality in the final product. Here are the essential traits to look for:

1. **Material Compatibility:** Ensure that the label sheets are compatible with the specific digital printing technology being used (e.g., inkjet or laser), as different materials perform differently with each type of printer.
2. **Print Quality:** Look for label sheets that offer high print resolution and clarity, enhancing the quality of the printed text and images. This is crucial for branding and marketing.
3. **Adhesive Quality:** Choose label sheets with strong, reliable adhesives that can adhere well to the intended surfaces (e.g., glass, plastic, metal) without peeling or curling, even over time or under varying environmental conditions.
4. **Durability:** Consider the durability of the label sheets, including resistance to moisture, UV exposure, and tearing. This is especially important for labels that will be used in challenging environments, such as outdoors or in refrigeration.
5. **Finish Options:** Evaluate the available finishes, such as matte, gloss, or satin, to ensure they align with the branding and aesthetic preferences of clients. The finish can significantly influence the look and feel of the final product.

6. **Thickness and Weight:** Choose an appropriate thickness and weight for the label sheets that match the application requirements, affecting factors like handling, application, and print quality.
7. **Eco-Friendliness:** Consider environmentally friendly options made from recycled materials or those that are biodegradable. Sustainability is increasingly important for many brands in their product packaging.
8. **Ease of Cutting and Handling:** Look for label sheets that are easy to handle, cut, and feed into the printer to minimize production downtime and improve efficiency in the printing process.
9. **Die-Cut Options:** Check if the label sheets are available in custom die-cut shapes, which can provide added value and versatility in applications, making them attractive for creative labeling solutions.
10. **Temperature Resistance:** For labels that will be exposed to extreme temperatures, ensure that the sheets can withstand those conditions without losing adhesion or print quality.
11. **Testing Samples:** Prioritize vendors that offer sample sheets for testing before bulk ordering. This allows for evaluation of print quality, adhesion, and durability under actual conditions.

By carefully considering these traits, a professional digital printer can select the right label sheets to meet client needs effectively, enhance printing capabilities, and ultimately contribute to the success of their labeling projects.

Resources and Further Reading

Comprehensive List of Resources

Industry Reports and Research Studies

- India Digital Printing Market Report by 6W Research
- Digital Printing Global Market Report by Yahoo Finance

Online Courses and Tutorials

- Digital Printing Course by the Indian Institute of Printing Technology
- Diploma in Printing Technology by the Indian Institute of Skill Development Training

Industry Magazines and Publications

- Print & Publishing
- Indian Printer and Publisher
- Press Idea

Conferences and Trade Shows

- PrintPack India
- IndiaCorr Expo
- PackPlus

Online Communities and Forums

- All India Digital Printers Association – AIDPA (Facebook group)
- PrintWeek (LinkedIn group)
- And many more...

These resources can provide valuable insights, information, and networking opportunities for those interested in exploring digital printing technologies in India.

❍ ❍ ❍ ❍

Ready, Set, Transform!

You've explored the exciting world of digital label printing—now it's time to put those insights into action and give your business a boost.

So, are you ready to take your business to the next level? Innovation is the key to unlocking new opportunities and staying ahead of the competition. By embracing innovative solutions, you can:

- **Improve Efficiency:** Streamline your operations and reduce costs.
- **Enhance Customer Experience:** Offer unique and personalized products that delight your customers.
- **Gain a Competitive Edge:** Differentiate your business from the competition and attract new customers.

Don't be afraid to try something new. Innovation can lead to unexpected rewards. Let's work together to explore the possibilities and build a brighter future for your business.

Address: N-10, Satyawati Nagar, Delhi-110 052.

Email: ashok@desmat.com **Or** archit@desmat.com

Regards,

Ashok Gupta & Archit Gupta